Sun of

The 10X Rule: The Only Difference between Success and Failure
Grant Cardone

Conversation Starters

By BookHabits

Please Note: This is an unofficial conversation starters guide. If you have not yet read the original work or would like to read it again, **get the book here.**

Copyright © 2017 by BookHabits. All Rights Reserved.
First Published in the United States of America 2017

We hope you enjoy this complementary guide from BookHabits.
Our mission is to aid readers and reading groups with quality, thought provoking material to in the discovery and discussions on some of today's favorite books.

Disclaimer / Terms of Use: Product names, logos, brands, and other trademarks featured or referred to within this publication are the property of their respective trademark holders and are not affiliated with BookHabits. The publisher and author make no representations or warranties with respect to the accuracy or completeness of these contents and disclaim all warranties such as warranties of fitness for a particular purpose. This guide is unofficial and unauthorized. It is not authorized, approved, licensed, or endorsed by the original book's author or publisher and any of their licensees or affiliates.

No part of this publication may be reproduced or retransmitted, electronic or mechanical, without the written permission of the publisher.

Tips for Using BookHabits Conversation Starters:

EVERY GOOD BOOK CONTAINS A WORLD FAR DEEPER THAN the surface of its pages. The characters and their world come alive through the words on the pages, yet the characters and its world still live on. Questions herein are designed to bring us beneath the surface of the page and invite us into the world that lives on. These questions can be used to:

- Foster a deeper understanding of the book
- Promote an atmosphere of discussion for groups
- Assist in the study of the book, either individually or corporately
- Explore unseen realms of the book as never seen before

About Us:

THROUGH YEARS OF EXPERIENCE AND FIELD EXPERTISE, from newspaper featured book clubs to local library chapters, *BookHabits* can bring your book discussion to life. Host your book party as we discuss some of today's most widely read books.

Table of Contents

Introducing *The 10X Rule: The Only Difference between Success and Failure* 6
Discussion Questions 14
Introducing the Author 35
Fireside Questions 41
Quiz Questions 52
Quiz Answers 65
Ways to Continue Your Reading 66

Introducing *The 10X Rule: The Only Difference between Success and Failure*

GRANT CARDONE HAS SPENT MANY YEARS STUDYING successful and unsuccessful people in order to better understand success and how it can be achieved. He says most people agree about the main aspects of success—setting goals, having discipline, managing your time, etc—but he wanted to know if there was "one thing" that can make the difference between success and failure. This questioning is what led to his creation of the 10X Rule, which, of course, is the basis for his latest book, *The 10X Rule: The Only Difference between Success and Failure.*

The book begins with an explanation of what the 10X Rule is and what it can do for you. The 10x Rule has two key parts—setting "massive goals" and taking "massive action." Cardone says that the 10X Rule will allow you to achieve more than you can ever possibly imagine in all aspects of your life. The author says the 10X Rule helps you understand the amount of effort it will require to successfully complete your goals. He says most people underestimate what it takes to successfully complete a goal, which is where the first part of the 10X Rule focuses—understanding exactly how much effort a particular goal will take.

According to Cardone, meeting goals, no matter how big, is hard work; so you should set your goals high—have "massive goals." The higher you set your goals, the more motivated you will be. The higher you aim, the higher you will hit. When planning for a project, you should expect it to take 10 times the effort and resources than you think, which will require more effort on your part, which leads us to the second part of the 10X Rule.

Setting your goals high is going to require you to take "massive action." Cardone says this is the part he has failed at in the past. He says you have to adjust your thinking so you can dream bigger. You should set out to take 10 times the action than most people would assume is necessary.

Cardone says that it doesn't matter how great your product or service is, chances are something is going to come up that you weren't prepared for—things like natural disasters, market fluctuations, political issues, medical emergencies, etc. The author says that the 10X Rule will prepare you for these types of "unexpected events."

In the book, Cardone discusses success in great detail. He begins by defining success, and in doing so points out that success usually looks different from person to person, depending on their age and station in life. He talks about different types of success in your personal life and professional life. The author presents you with a list of what he considers to be the most crucial things you need to know about success, including its importance and the abundance of success available to people, and more.

One of the things on Cardone's list is your duty when it comes to success. He says he decided to stop waiting for success and began seeing it as his duty to his future, his family, and his employer. Cardone mentions that he was disappointed in the fact that no one ever taught him about success in all his years in school.

Cardone's list says "there is no shortage of success." The author says that success has no limits—all it takes is things like creativity, determination, ingenuity, etc. He says too many people see success as a limited resource, but that's just not true, according to him. He believes there can be multiple winners. He doesn't believe you acquire success; he believes you have to create it for yourself.

Cardone feels very strongly about taking responsibility for your success. He actually contemplated calling one of the chapters of the book, "Don't Be a Little Bitch," but decided against it so as to not offend anyone. In that particular chapter, which he calls, "Assume Control for Everything," he says that people who make excuses are unable to create success. He says you have to take responsibility and accept accountability—no excuses!

Cardone defines four degrees of action in his book—1) Do nothing, 2) Retreat, 3) Take normal levels of action, and 4) Take massive action. He believes that your chances of getting a break increase with the amount of action you are willing to take. He says you will use each of these levels in different aspects of your life. For example, you may put more "action" into your career than you are willing to put into your community. Cardone spends several chapters describing each of these degrees of action and how they affect your life.

The 10X Rule has fared well with readers and critics alike. Brian Tracy, bestselling author of over 45 books, said the author "hit the nail on the head" when it comes to revealing the reason people are successful in life. Bestselling author Larry Winget said that "the 10X Rule is dead on right."

Discussion Questions

"Get Ready to Enter a New World"

Tip: Begin with questions dealing with broader issues to ensure ample time for quality discussions. Read through all discussion questions before engaging.

~~~

question 1

The book begins with an explanation of what the 10X Rule is and what it can do for you. In your own words, define the 10X Rule.

~~~

question 2

The author says the 10X Rule helps you understand the amount of effort it will require to successfully complete your goals. He says most people underestimate what it takes to successfully complete a goal. Tell about a time when you underestimated the effort a particular task would take. How did the book help you understand better how to plan for a goal?

~~~

question 3

The author says you should have "massive goals." In your own words, define massive goal.

~~~

~~~

question 4

The author also refers to "massive action." What does the author mean by massive action?

~~~

~~~

question 5

The author admits to having failed at taking action in his life. Tell about a time when you failed because you didn't take enough action in completing your goal.

~~~

~~~

question 6

The author says that it doesn't matter how great your product or service is, chances are something is going to come up that you weren't prepared for. Tell about something that could, or has, come up that distracted you from your goal or caused you to fail.

~~~

~~~

question 7

Cardone points out that success usually looks different from person to person, depending on their age and station in life. How would you define success in your life?

~~~

~~~

question 8

The author presents you with a list of what he considers to be the most crucial things you need to know about success. Tell the one item from his list spoke to you the most and why?

~~~

~~~

question 9

The author doesn't believe you acquire success; he believes you have to create it for yourself. How do you view success in this regard, and why?

~~~

~~~

question 10

Cardone mentions that he was disappointed in the fact that no one ever taught him about success in all his years in school. Were you taught anything about success in school? Why do you think most children are not?

~~~

question 11

The author says that success has no limits—all it takes is things like creativity, determination, ingenuity, etc. He says too many people see success as a limited resource, but that's just not true, according to him. Before reading the book, did you see success as a "limited resource"? Why do you think so many people do?

question 12

Cardone contemplated calling one of the chapters of the book, "Don't Be a Little Bitch," but decided against it so as to not offend anyone. Would this chapter title have offended you? Why or why not? Why do you think it may offend others?

question 13

Cardone defines four degrees of action in his book—1) Do nothing, 2) Retreat, 3) Take normal levels of action, and 4) Take massive action. He says you will use each of these levels in different aspects of your life. Do you think you should be at a level 4 in all areas of your life? Why or why not?

question 14

Thinking about these four degrees of action, where would you rate yourself in terms of your professional life, and why?

~~~

question 15

What degree of action would you rate your spiritual life, and why?

~~~

~~~

question 16

Brian Tracy said Cardone "hit the nail on the head" when it comes to revealing the reason people are successful in life, and Larry Winget said that "the 10X Rule is dead on right." Do you agree with their opinion about the content of the book? Why or why not?

~~~

question 17

Some say the book is more appropriate for sales professional instead of entrepreneurs. Do you agree or do you think it is good advice for both? Explain.

~ ~ ~

question 18

Many reviewers have said that the book is a great motivational tool. Do you agree? Why or why not?

~ ~ ~

~~~

question 19

The 10X Rule does not seem to be doing as well as *You're Either First, or You're Last.* Compare and contrast these two books.

~~~

~~~

question 20

Some reviewers say that the book is basic and tells information that most already know. Do you agree? Why or why not? Tell about one thing you learned from the book.

~~~

Introducing the Author

GRANT CARDONE IS A *NEW YORK TIMES* bestselling author, speaker, sales training expert, and real estate investor. He is also known for his radio show called *The Cardone Show* and has appeared on television as well.

Cardone was born in 1958 in Lake Charles, Louisiana to Curtis and Concetta Cardone. He has four siblings, including a twin brother named Gary. He attended LaGrange High School and eventually went on to study accounting at McNeese State University, where he received his bachelor's degree.

He began his career in Chicago as an employee of a sales training company. Over his career, he has lived in various parts of the U.S., including Texas, California, and Florida. In those various places, he has held a variety of jobs, including accounting and automobile sales positions before venturing out as an entrepreneur.

Cardone owns several of his own businesses, most of which are sales-training companies. He specializes in helping companies of all sizes grow by helping them find missed opportunities and improve sales processes. He teaches his clients and followers to take responsibility for their own success and encourages them to "rise above outdated, unworkable middle-class myths and limitations" so that they can experience "true freedom." He is straightforward when it comes to offering advice about leadership, economics, and business. He is sought after by the media for his opinions and expertise on the important topics in business.

Cardone has created sales training programs for a variety of companies and individuals. In 2010, he started the Grant Cardone Sales Training University and the Grant Cardone On-Demand Automotive Sales Training programs. Both programs are leaders in the web-based sales training industry.

Cardone's website, training programs, books, etc., all feature his expertise and advice in the areas of sales, marketing, branding, and entrepreneurship. He even offers apps to his fans and readers of his books—*Close the Sale*, which was designed to help salespeople in particular selling situation; *10X VIP* gives users access to Cardone's events, products, and services; and *My GCTV* offers users sales training and business tips.

Cardone's fans can also access *Grant Cardone TV*, which is an entrepreneur network that offers videos featuring Mr. Cardone, including *Whatever it Takes, Young Hustlers, Confessions of an Entrepreneur, Real Estate Investing,* to name a few. Cardone developed a reality show called *Turnaround King* for the National Geographic Channel. He makes regular appearances on both the

Fox News Channel and Fox Business Channel, as well as CNBC and MSNBC. He also contributes to the *Huffington Post* and *Entreprenuer.com* on a regular basis.

Cardone has written seven books about sales and business, including *Sell to Survive* (2008), *If You're Not First, You're Last* (2010), *The Closer's Survival Guide* (2011), *The 10X Rule* (2011), *Sell or Be Sold* (2012), *The Millionaire Booklet* (2016), and *Be Obsessed or Be Average* (2016).

Today, it is estimated that Grant Cardone is worth $300 million dollars. He is very active on social media with over one million Facebook followers, more than 500 thousand Instagram followers, and over 400 thousand Twitter followers.

Cardone is married to Elena Lyons and has two daughters, Scarlett and Sabrina.

Fireside Questions

"What would you do?"

Tip: These questions can be a fun exercise as it spurs creativity among the readers by allowing alternate scene endings and "if this was you" questions.

~~~

question 21

Over his career, the Cardone has lived in various parts of the U.S. and has held a variety of jobs. How do you think the diversity of homes and jobs has helped him become successful in his career?

~~~

~~~

question 22

Cardone is straightforward when it comes to offering advice about leadership, economics, and business. What do you think of this style of writing and teaching?

~~~

~~~

question 23

Cardone is sought after by the media for his opinions and expertise on the important topics in business. What do you think it is about Cardone that makes him so popular?

~~~

~~~

question 24

Cardone offers apps to his fans and readers of his books—*Close the Sale, 10X VIP,* and *My GCTV.* Which of these apps have you used, and what is your opinion of the usefulness of the app.

~~~

~~~

question 25

Cardone has written seven books about sales and business. Which is your favorite, and why?

~~~

~~~

question 26

The author spends a lot of time in the book discussing success—the meaning, the importance, the benefits, etc. If you were writing a similar book, would you have chosen to spend so much time on success? What would be your main focus, and why?

~~~

~~~

question 27

The author contemplated calling one of the chapters of the book, "Don't Be a Little Bitch," but decided against it so as to not offend anyone. Would you have used this chapter title? Why or why not?

~~~

~~~

question 28

The 10X Rule was written by Grant Cardone, a male. How do you think the book would be different if it had been written by a female author?

~~~

~~~

question 29

The book seemed to focus heavily on the effort that one puts into an idea rather than coming up with good ideas. If you were writing the book, which would you focus more on—effort and hard work or coming up with good ideas and intelligence? Why?

~~~

question 30

The book seems to be written to a general audience, whereas Cardone's other books were written to specific audiences—salespeople, entrepreneurs, etc. Would you have chosen to write to a wider audience or focus on a more specific audience, and why?

~~~

Quiz Questions

"Ready to Announce the Winners?"

Tip: Create a leaderboard and track scores to see who gets the most correct answers. Winners required. Prizes optional.

~~~

quiz question 1

The 10x Rule has two key parts: setting _____ and taking _____.

~~~

~~~

quiz question 2

When planning for a project, you should expect it to take _____the effort and resources than you think

~~~

~~~

quiz question 3

True or false: the author says he has failed when it comes to taking action.

~~~

~~~

quiz question 4

True or False: the author spends a few chapters defining failure and how it affects people.

~~~

~~~

quiz question 5

The author says he decided to stop waiting for success and began seeing it as his _____ to his future, his family, and his employer.

~~~

~~~

quiz question 6

True or False: the author is very grateful that his teachers in school taught him about success.

~~~

~~~

quiz question 7

True or False: the author says success is limited, so you must be competitive and move quickly in your field.

~~~

~~~

quiz question 8

The author began his career in Chicago as an employee of a _____.

~~~

~~~

quiz question 9

_____ is an entrepreneur network that offers videos featuring the author.

~~~

~~~

quiz question 10

The author developed a reality show called _____for the National Geographic Channel.

~~~

~~~

quiz question 11

True or False: *The 10X Rule* is the author's first and only attempt at writing a full-length book.

~~~

~~~

quiz question 12

It is estimated that Grant Cardone is worth _____ dollars.

~~~

Quiz Answers

1. goals; action
2. ten times
3. true
4. False; he spends a few chapters defining and discussing success.
5. duty
6. False; he was disappointed that no one ever taught him about success in all his years in school.
7. False; The author says that success has no limits
8. sales training company
9. Grant Cardone TV
10. Turnaround King
11. False; he has written a total of seven full-length books
12. 300 million

Ways to Continue Your Reading

EVERY month, our team runs through a wide selection of books to pick the best titles for readers and reading groups, and promotes these titles to our thousands of readers – sometimes with free downloads, sale dates, and additional brochures.

If you have not yet read the original work or would like to read it again, get the book here.

Want to register yourself or a book group? It's free and takes 1-click.

Register here.

On the Next Page...

Please write us your reviews! Any length would be fine but we'd appreciate hearing you more! We'd be SO grateful.

Till next time,

BookHabits

"Loving Books is Actually a Habit"

CPSIA information can be obtained
at www.ICGtesting.com
Printed in the USA
LVHW041719071120
671047LV00002B/320